Praise for *Pony*

MW00942622

"In sharing his own mystic journey, Hedin Daubenspeck has provided a one-stop introduction of the beliefs, philosophies, and practices available for enlightenment.

Regardless of where one is on their spiritual path and search for more information to deepen their understanding, they will find *Pony Ride to an Awakening* an easy read, filled with information of ancient and current spiritual practices.

I would recommend it to beginners as well as long time travelers ready to take their next step."

— Rev. S. Culliver Brookman, minister
(Unity World Ministries)

"What is man, that Thou art mindful of him?" the Psalmist wrote — and captured what may be that most persistent and profound question of all humanity. What are you, really? What potentials do humans have and what is your nature? Some never wrestle with those questions, but for some it is a compelling three-in-the-morning question.

Pony Ride to an Awakening is a chronicle of the search for an answer. Freemasonry is not the only institution to encourage its members to look deeply within, but it is one of the few which sees that search as a quest rather than a position of dogma. Whether you call it esoteric, the metaphysical, or by some other name, the experience and search for the spiritual aspect of our being is common to most of us and has been, at least since the time of the painted caves.

Here we have one man's hero's journey — the call to

adventure, the quest, the enlightenment, and the return. And it is the return — the bringing back what has been found for the benefit of others — which informs the book. Each person's journey is unique, of course, but each also shares the basic elements. Our author has studied and learned (and continues to learn) what the sages have taught, and makes it available to the reader.

Knowledge and wisdom are different things. New knowledge often supplants old. Little of Aristotle's science is taught today save as the history of ideas. But his wisdom, his philosophy, is as valuable as ever. In a similar way, the writings of those who explored human spirituality have the same validity as signposts for us as they had for their contemporaries. The author has given us the signposts expressed in the understanding and vocabulary of our time. That is a valuable service in an age in which there is an awakening sense that we are missing something and that it is something which rests within ourselves."

— Jim Tresnor, Grand Orator
(Grand Lodge of Oklahoma)

"Hedin Daubenspeck shows us how to make the 'perennial spiritual wisdom' or 'golden thread' come alive for us as we face difficult decisions—on both the personal and the global levels—in the 21st century."

— Rev. Dr. Richard Belous, Senior
Minister (Unity Center of Tulsa)

PONY RIDE
TO AN
AWAKENING
THE JOURNEY OF A MYSTIC

HEDIN E. DAUBENSPECK

BALBOA.PRESS
A DIVISION OF HAY HOUSE

Copyright © 2020 Hedin E. Daubenspeck.

All rights reserved. No part of this book may be used or reproduced by any means,
graphic, electronic, or mechanical, including photocopying, recording, taping or by
any information storage retrieval system without the written permission of the author
except in the case of brief quotations embodied in critical articles and reviews.

Balboa Press books may be ordered through booksellers or by contacting:

Balboa Press
A Division of Hay House
1663 Liberty Drive
Bloomington, IN 47403
www.balboapress.com
1 (877) 407-4847

Because of the dynamic nature of the Internet, any web addresses or
links contained in this book may have changed since publication and
may no longer be valid. The views expressed in this work are solely those
of the author and do not necessarily reflect the views of the publisher,
and the publisher hereby disclaims any responsibility for them.

The author of this book does not dispense medical advice or prescribe the use
of any technique as a form of treatment for physical, emotional, or medical
problems without the advice of a physician, either directly or indirectly. The
intent of the author is only to offer information of a general nature to help you
in your quest for emotional and spiritual well-being. In the event you use any
of the information in this book for yourself, which is your constitutional right,
the author and the publisher assume no responsibility for your actions.

Any people depicted in stock imagery provided by Getty Images are
models, and such images are being used for illustrative purposes only.
Certain stock imagery © Getty Images.

Edited by J T Hinds, theimpeccableeditor.com
Cover Design Nicole Martini
Author Photo by Amy Teague Portraits
Interior Image Credit Ariel Mulvaney
Interior Image Credit Erwin Newton

ISBN: 978-1-9822-4335-7 (sc)
ISBN: 978-1-9822-4336-4 (hc)
ISBN: 978-1-9822-4337-1 (e)

Library of Congress Control Number: 2020903113

Printed in the United States of America.

Balboa Press rev. date: 07/15/2020

CONTENTS

This book is dedicated to my mother and father
for their unconditional love and support.

Hedin on his Shetland pony, Fury,
while growing up on the family farm.

That which I seek, I am.

ACKNOWLEDGMENTS

I am grateful to the following people who have played important roles in my personal spiritual development and in the writing of this book.

Dana, my wife, for being lovingly patient over the many hours I have dedicated to this book and for her loving support and encouragement. Thank you for sharing in this riverboat ride of life.

Without the aid of my spirit teachers and guides on the inner planes, this book would not have been possible. I acknowledge the teachers in spirit and angels who have helped me, including the archangels, thrones, and cherubim.

Debra Merkes, intuitive guide, for her many soul readings and for her contribution to this book.

The following Unity World Ministry ministers who influenced my spiritual development. John Rankin, Sig Paulson, and Howard Caesar (Unity's Golden Pyramid of Light in Houston), Culliver Brookman (co-founder with me of The

Center of Light Church), and Ann Marie Beale and Dr. Rick Belous (Unity Center of Tulsa).

The earthly spiritual teachers and intuitive friends in my life who have guided my learning and understanding, especially Grace Godwin, who always believed in me and offered encouragement in the many steps of my journey, including teaching and writing.

The following for their input: Arlene Chemers, Tom Culver, Monica McIntyre, Linda Grant, De Maris Gaines, Andrea Laney, Ray Daily, Jerry Newton, Alan Morrow, Allen Thomas, Jodi Tuttle, Gina Pearson, Wendy Berezowski, Peggy Ewing, Pam Herod, Donna Beth Ingersoll, Liz Gore, Tyra Langley, Kathy Brennan, Lee Warren, and Shelly Huffman.

PREFACE

My awakening as a teenager aroused in me a yearning for greater understanding and was a turning point in my life. I offer this book as a guide for those seeking spiritual awareness in the hope that my recollections may inspire others in their efforts to awaken higher consciousness. I share reflections, practices, and beliefs that have shaped my spiritual understanding. I have included references to books that were helpful in validating my experiences. The mystical journey that I describe is an inner journey that leads to self-realization. I have undertaken the journey and so have many others. This journey involves spiritual awakening and going within.

Encounters with the spiritual realm have been reported throughout history. (Negative forces also exist in the universe but normally these cannot psychically influence people of good will, love, and happiness who use some type of protection, such as surrounding themselves with white light.) Our teachers, guides, and ancestors communicate with us to give guidance, wisdom, and vision. We come from Spirit and we will return to Spirit. Denial of spiritual and psychic experiences only shuts the door to wisdom and insight from Spirit. Reading about my psychic and spiritual experiences may help you trust your own experiences as real and not imagined.

This book is intended for people of all ages and backgrounds. You may understand part but not all of this writing in one reading. Don't be concerned about understanding all of it. Accept what you are ready to accept. Your understanding will broaden as you develop greater awareness.

We are closest to Spirit when we are just entering incarnation and at the end of life, but communication with the unseen world can happen at any time and any age. A distraught mother might ask a spirit guide to help find a lost child, while an elder at the end of life may visit with deceased family members who are helping to prepare the way for his transition. Altered states of consciousness and other mystical experiences sometimes occur as a portal opens in our psychic body.

Psychic senses in early childhood, such as having a friend or playmate that others cannot see, often diminishes as we are introduced to worldly knowledge. Increased awareness of the subtle realms often coincides with a "dark night of the soul" experience following the loss of a loved one, an emotional trauma, or a serious illness or accident.

It has been almost taboo in our culture for people to acknowledge disembodied spirits, even though we will all enter another realm when we die. Some people are more comfortable believing that psychic experiences originate from Jesus and/or God. Nevertheless, nomenclature does not make these incidents any less real. My writings recognize God, Jesus, and teachers and ancestors in spirit.

God gave direct commands to Adam, Noah, Moses, and Jesus, to name a few. I like to look at the visions of Ezekiel as being from a divine source. God continues to speak to us in modern times. In some modern spiritual traditions, developing a personal relationship with God is normal. Hearing voices and having visions can be an accepted part of the spiritual experience.

Much confusion exists about what occurs after death. I believe that consciousness continues after the death of the physical body. Belief in the continuation of consciousness beyond this life can give hope to those who fear death.

When we open our eyes and our minds, new aspects of truth unfold like a blossoming flower. As our understanding changes, new petals open. When our minds expand in awareness, the old truth changes to reveal new perspectives.

As we listen to the inner impressions coming forth from the silence, we learn to follow our intuition. As we follow our intuition, we balance our earthly existence and our spiritual reality.

INTRODUCTION

As a mystic and a student of the world's wisdom and religious teachings for many years, my insights and observations have been woven into a fabric of inner knowing. Here is an overview of what you will find in the chapters that follow. Italics indicate words found in the glossary.

Chapter 1, "Early Childhood," provides background about my early days growing up on a farm in southwestern Oklahoma. This was a time of experiencing nature while working on the farm and riding horses. I was introduced to the Christian religion and attended Sunday school.

In Chapter 2, "Pony Ride to an Awakening," I share an experience that occurred while riding horseback in the pasture — a turning point in my adolescence that inspired me to seek greater wisdom and understanding.

Chapter 3, "Psychic and Spiritual Experiences," explores various spiritual experiences that people have reported.

Chapter 4, "Finding the Light," is about gaining esoteric knowledge and finding the light within.

In Chapter 5, "Our Energy Bodies," I discuss the invisible bodies and higher senses. This chapter presents terms that are commonly used in describing spiritual concepts.

Those who hold positions of authority sometimes misuse their power, even in the ministry. Chapter 6, "Spiritual Abuse and Abuse of Spirit," serves as a reminder that we all must stay vigilant about the ways we use our spiritual gifts.

In Chapter 7, "A Shamanic Crisis," I share my own "dark night of the soul," an experience that brought me to my knees but also caused me to renew my relationship with God.

In Chapter 8, "Spirit Guides," I give examples of my communications with my guides to demonstrate the importance of our invisible helpers, who teach and encourage us.

In Chapter 9, "The Fourth Noble Truth: The Eightfold Path," I discuss the Buddhist practice of the Eightfold Path, which has been meaningful personally and which I highly endorse.

Meditation is an important technique for getting in touch with the inner voice. In Chapter 10, "Silence: Beyond Brain Chatter," I describe the process of going within to hear the inner voice.

In Chapter 11, "Consciousness between Death and Rebirth," I describe the death experience from an esoteric perspective and include information on the process of dying and what occurs during the time between death and rebirth.

In the final chapter, "Conclusion: What Now?," I offer encouragement and advice about how to have a happy and prosperous life.

Consciousness expands over a lifetime of experiential moments. When we can view these moments from a spiritual perspective, our understanding deepens and our lives are enriched.

ONENESS MANDALA

This unnamed painting is part of my personal collection of artwork.

In 1986, I spontaneously drew an image on a napkin while sitting at my breakfast table. I had been invited by the artist to visit her studio to observe a painting in progress. It was identical to my drawing. I bought it from the artist because I could see the symbolism of the sun, God, and consciousness, among other things, in this work. This painting has been useful in my own meditations.

Perhaps it symbolizes conception out of the cosmos. Does the lighter color at the top indicate a more enlightened state? When we focus our attention on the painting, we can gain insight and understanding.

ABOUT THE ARTIST

Airiel Mulvaney

Born and formed in Houston, Texas, Airiel received a Master of Fine Arts degree in studio arts from the University of California at Berkeley.

Feeling inundated with the objective images so prevalent in the advertising business, she chose to create works and art installations that are subjective and also experiential in nature. Her desire was and is to create work that can be sensed as well as seen: the mystery, the mystical, and the unknown.

Airiel now resides in the San Francisco Bay area where she paints and art directs. She said:

> My paintings are about space, quiet, chaos, and the unknown. An expression on canvas, paper or wood that is a dance between the inner world and the physical, always with the intention to bring forth what is unseen.
>
> Each series is an ongoing process seeking the point where inner meets outer with a desire to create a physical expression to what is unknowable, and yet palpable.
>
> Painting moves me into a primal mode, the reptilian, instinctual part of me is fully present and conscious, cautious, careful me is gone.

I grab paints, and mix right on the canvas, abandoning the brush and allowing the paint to find its place. I capture what is there — the elements or energies that move within space.

— Airiel Mulvaney

Meditation

Choose a quiet place and time when you will not be interrupted.

Begin by sitting in a comfortable, open-bodied posture. Keep your spine straight and your arms open.

Find a state of quiet peace and joy undisturbed by life's problems.

Focus on an image or on your breathing.

Take a deep breath.

Be aware of your breath as you breathe in.

Be aware of your breath as you breathe out.

Sit quietly for a while until your mind becomes calm.

Sit in the silence until you enter a state of quiescence.

Watch your thoughts and let them pass by without giving them attention or emotional energy.

Set aside 20 minutes each day to meditate.

> (With daily practice, one can learn to maintain mindfulness twenty-four hours a day, even while busy with other tasks or working.)

> In this meditative state of mind, open to receiving, begin reading the next section.

MORNING MEDITATION

Waking to an idea in the morning is a wonderful way to start the day. A few years ago, I awoke to the following message in my mind, which provided an excellent focus for my morning meditation.

From the unseen, we become manifest. This manifestation is the beginning of existence. The will to live and the longing for life accompany existence. We take our first breath. From this beginning we become aware of consciousness, that which is and always was. Consciousness brings awareness of self. With awareness, we see opposites: male and female; light and dark; good and evil.

At first, we see duality of opposites externally, outside of ourselves; then we see that opposites are also within. When we experience separation, we are lost from the truth. As we reconcile and find harmony that incorporates these differences, we overcome separation. Living in harmony, we find that we are one with all life.

While meditating, we may go beyond mind and thoughts to the silence in the space of No Mind. In this emptiness, we find higher awareness and bliss. Here, we hear the voice of God and receive divine wisdom. We realize that God is within. Our ideas become manifest as we create.

CHAPTER 1

EARLY CHILDHOOD

J ust as individuals have different physical abilities, they also
have different psychic abilities. Sometimes our talents and
abilities come down through family lines. For example, some
families have a long line of members who practice medicine or
play music or paint. My gift of psychic perception, which we
all have to some degree, came from my mother's side and from
my father's side.

I have vague memories of my paternal grandmother, who
died when I was three. My grandmother lived with my dad and
his two brothers on their farm until my dad married in 1948.
Thereafter, she continued to live with my uncles, Eugene and
Noel. (My paternal grandfather died in 1918 of the Spanish
influenza.)

One of my cousins recently shared with me a story about
our grandmother's psychic abilities. During World War II, the

Army would not disclose the whereabouts of service members to family members. My grandmother told the family that my dad was in French Morocco. She said the Lord told her where he was. After the war, my dad confirmed he had been assigned to a hospital in Casablanca.

My mother was also psychic and consulted an intuitive from time to time to confirm her own knowing. (This was especially true when my oldest brother was in Vietnam.) Like my mother and my grandmother, I've had psychic abilities all my life. As a child, I thought everyone had these kinds of abilities. It wasn't until I got older that I realized I was different than other people.

I was born three months premature. (I weighed less than three pounds. My first baby bed was a shoebox.) According to Manly P. Hall, a child born in the seventh month is often psychically "sensitive" and may not be as tightly bound to the body as full-term babies.[1] Perhaps my premature birth had been planned in the invisible plane before I was conceived, for developing my psychic awareness has been an important part of my life.

Children can sometimes be observed talking to invisible friends, who are as real to them as human friends and animal friends. (Some children develop psychic abilities as a way to escape into the unseen world when they experience trauma early in life.) Children understand fairy tales without needing interpretation because, as Swiss psychiatrist and psychoanalyst Carl Jung explained, archetypes exist in our subconscious

---

[1] Manly P. Hall, *Man: The Grand Symbol of the Mysteries*, 6th ed. (1932; repr., Los Angeles: Philosophical Research Society, 1972), 115–116.

mind. Ideas about a prince and princess, a trickster, or a wise old man surface from the unconscious.

A gifted child may foresee the birth of a sibling or the death of a relative, and some children experience astral travel (during sleep or while awake). Significant dreams from childhood can continue to be of importance later in life.

I grew up on a farm in southwestern Oklahoma. In the 1950s, we had electricity but no television or air conditioning. Each evening, my family would sit on the back porch to stay cool. My parents pointed to the constellations as my three brothers and I gazed into the night sky. My father said he believed life forms must exist on other planets. Our nightly ritual gave me a feeling of *oneness* with the universe.

Typical of farm families in Oklahoma and the Midwest, my family attended the local church, which, in our case, was a Baptist church. Sunday school teachers spoke of a separate God, which I imagined as a male God up in the sky.

Salvation was at the core of the Baptist teachings. To belong to the church, one had to be baptized, profess a belief in Jesus, and make a lifetime membership commitment. Then and only then could one be assured of salvation and entrance into Heaven upon death.

My rite of passage was a spiritual crisis, not one concerning puberty or sexuality. I felt a split between my natural connection with Divine Source and the pressure to assimilate the church's teachings. The church's presentation of a separate God was in conflict with my sense of the interconnectedness of all things. I had difficulty believing that we are all born sinners in need of redemption. I was also stumbling over the teaching that on Judgment Day the wrath of God would fall upon those who had not been "saved." It seemed incomprehensible to me that so many people who believed differently could receive God's wrath. My God was a loving God.

I was, by nature, a spiritual child. I wanted to belong, not set myself apart. My fear that I could not live up to my family's expectations caused me great anxiety. So, at the age of twelve I went forward in the church and became baptized, trying to fit in and hoping this step would lay my questions to rest. It did not. I still felt torn.

This was a tumultuous time in my life as I tried to find peace within myself while feeling confused. I did not feel comfortable discussing my internal conflicts with my parents. (They did not discuss their views about spiritual matters very often.) Nor could I share my experience of God with the church elders. (Not having the knowledge to refute the church teachings, I did not have any basis for disagreeing with them.) If I had been able to articulate my feelings to my parents and elders, I might have been able to resolve my conflicts, but I was afraid I would be shunned.

My foundational morals and ethics derived from the influence of my parents and my maternal grandparents, with whom I spent a lot of time in my early childhood. Religious education was, for me, more a distraction and an annoyance than a blessing. I had to learn the church's teachings and then unlearn them.

No one religion holds all of life's answers. Nature is intelligent and an unbiased teacher. If we learn and understand the lessons of the natural world, we can find harmony within ourselves in the midst of the turns and twists of life.

CHAPTER 2

PONY RIDE TO AN AWAKENING

At the age of thirteen, I had a spiritual experience in nature that changed the course of my life and set me on a new path. I was riding my quarter horse, Little Red, bareback in the pasture one bright afternoon, as I often did. It was early spring, and the pasture was covered with purple wildflowers. The intense fragrance of the wildflowers, along with the rhythmic movement of the quarter horse, stimulated all my senses and aroused in me a profound sense of ecstasy. Intoxicated by the beauty of the day, I felt at one with nature, God, and the universe, in tune with the infinite. For the first time in my life, I felt whole.

I couldn't explain my innate sense of oneness with all life, but I knew that life is sacred. As I went through puberty, I felt carefree, for by this time my conflicts about church dogma were mostly suppressed and forgotten. The experience I had in the pasture helped me trust my inner guidance. It awakened me to Spirit and showed me a path beyond the teachings of my church. By listening to the voice within, I was able to reject the strict Baptist edicts without the guilt, shame, and fear that had earlier tormented me.

The Abrahamic religions (Judaism, Islam, and Christianity) teach that God and humans are separate. This belief creates a perception of an uncaring God that exists outside of humanity, a God people pray to for forgiveness and blessings. The spontaneous *numinous* experience of nature awakened in me a higher consciousness. I was now able to understand what Jesus meant when he said, "The Father and I are One." The higher self (united with God's will) has overcome the lower self (personal will). Jesus's message was that all mankind could experience Christ consciousness, as he did. This union is the true salvation.

In my early twenties, I discovered Unity Worldwide Ministries. Unity takes a more metaphysical approach to the Bible than the Baptist church of my youth. I also found the writings of Manly P. Hall, founder of the Philosophical Research Society. Hall's method of analysis was helpful in my spiritual development.

Although I study the wisdom teachings found in all cultures for spiritual insight, through my early church attendance I learned the stories, books, and organization of the Bible. As with myth, the wisdom of the Torah and the Bible is often buried beneath allegory, which I have learned to interpret for myself by looking at the story behind the story.

A message I received from Spirit while taking courses at the University of Philosophical Research in my sixties was that God is omnipresent. This message helped me understand intellectually what had occurred while riding horseback in the pasture. I had connected with Divine Source.

CHAPTER 3

PSYCHIC AND SPIRITUAL EXPERIENCES

Perhaps you know someone who is gifted with intuitive abilities, or perhaps you yourself have psychic abilities that you draw upon in everyday life. Extrasensory perception, or *ESP*, is the nonphysical "sixth sense."[2] Advanced spiritual understanding goes beyond simply having psychic abilities, however. Psychic abilities aid conscious awareness, but one must be able to interpret the psychic experiences in spiritual terms to gain the most understanding.

Intuition, one form of ESP, is an important part of a spiritual life. The more I learned to trust my intuition and follow the guidance of my spirit teachers, the more harmonious my life became.

---

[2] The five physical senses are sight, smell, taste, hearing, and touch.

Sometimes the messages I get pertain to mundane things. For example, my intuition once told me to change watches as I was getting dressed for work. I ignored the message and at ten in the morning my watch stopped working. The battery was dead. I was reminded of the importance of paying attention to my guidance.

Another time, as I was waiting at the café counter in a grocery store with my son and daughter to buy ice cream, and I became aware of the voice of an infant in my inner ear. (I don't know how I knew it was an infant, but I knew.) The voice asked (telepathically) that I come to the milk department.

The three of us proceeded to walk to the milk department, where I found a baby in a shopping cart near his mother. The baby had cerebral palsy and possibly other conditions. The mother was watching me as I watched the baby, so I spoke to her of the baby's condition. She told me she and her husband were almost bankrupt from the child's medical expenses.

As a member of Shriners International, an appendant body to Freemasonry, I knew of a free Masonic hospital for children. I told the mother I would assist her in gaining admission for her child. This was the first time I can remember having an experience of *telepathy*. (When you are thinking about someone and the phone rings, as that person is attempting to reach you, you are connecting with each other telepathically.)

You may at times have the sense that you are being guided in your choices. You are inspired to follow a certain course of action — to draw a picture or lay out the framework for a contract or take a certain trip or class. You may be browsing in a bookstore when your intuition guides you to exactly the right book, which you may not have been aware of otherwise. You might have a hunch about stopping in a store, and when you do, you find that an item you have been wanting is on sale. Over time, you learn that trusting your hunches leads to positive outcomes.

The more you listen and the more you trust and follow your intuition, the more you have access to seemingly magical power. You might not have the awareness to understand the process by which these things are happening, but you are receiving inspired guidance. Conscious understanding may come later— perhaps during meditation.

NEAR DEATH EXPERIENCES

We sometimes hear about the spiritual experiences of others, such as the sight of a recently deceased loved one standing in a doorway or at the foot of the bed. The *spirit realm* is always beside us, but we tend to forget that in daily life.

People who have had a near-death experience (NDE) often tell of encountering a messenger or guide or a departed loved one after leaving the body. Perhaps an adverse event occurred during surgery and the individual was conscious of viewing his body on the operating table or some other medical emergency precipitated the NDE.

Seeing a bright light is often a part of the NDE experience, as is feeling an overwhelming sense of love. Some individuals are told they must finish their earthly mission; they are not yet ready to transition. When they awaken, they retain the memory of the experience and often have more respect for life, having been given a second chance. Their new lives are filled with meaning and purpose.

DREAMS AND DÉJÀ VU

Many of us receive messages from dreams. A dream may foretell of coming events, such as the birth of a child. In 1992, while living in Houston, I sensed the presence of a spirit in my home. I was very curious why this spirit was present with me. About a month later, my twenty-two-year-old stepdaughter, who was not married at the time, told me at the breakfast table that she was pregnant. I knew then that the spirit that had been lingering in my home was her baby boy. I felt happy and told her she should have the baby. I felt great love for this child as I held him in my arms after his birth.

Our ancestors sometimes visit us in our dreams. They may warn us of danger or help us prepare for the passing of a loved one. Throughout life we have dreams that contain important messages, though we may not always remember the dreams or understand the messages. We can also be aware of activities occurring on the *astral plane* during sleep. These are called lucid dreams. Developing continuity of consciousness is evidence of spiritual growth.

When an eighty-year-old friend told me she dreamed of being asked to hold an infant while it underwent heart surgery on the spiritual plane, I sensed that the baby was still in the womb. A healer once told me that she assists transitioning souls who have passed over following an emergency, such as an earthquake or other disaster. She helps these souls to gain an understanding of what has occurred and to realize that they have passed into spirit. She has the conscious awareness of helping during her sleep.

Another common psychic experience is *déjà vu*, the feeling that we have been somewhere before or met someone before. I saw a woman at a dance in 1974 and felt an instant sense of recognition, though we had never met. She became my wife and gave me two children, for which I feel blessed. We were married for almost ten years. Sometimes past life memories are behind these experiences. If so, they can be accessed through hypnosis or regression therapy.

EMPATHS

An empath is affected by other people's energies and intuitively feels their emotional and physical states in exactly the same way as the person in pain or distress (whereas a clairsentient receives information about a person's energy from objects and locations). For example, during a spiritual group meeting, I once felt someone's bladder pain in my body in exactly the same place as the person having the pain. These experiences can be confusing until the empath learns to discern and separate his own feelings from those of another. Talking things out can help you identify which feelings are yours.

Psychic Healing

I once consulted a psychic healer to help me determine the cause of a pain in my spleen. He found a *discarnate entity* attached to my spleen and encouraged the entity to release and move on. The pain immediately stopped. Psychic healing often occurs on the *etheric* level. (I discuss the etheric body in greater detail in Chapter 4.)

Intuition and Increasing Psychic Awareness

As our intuitive abilities are strengthened, the door to spiritual guidance opens. We learn how to achieve more harmony in our lives, even in the midst of difficult circumstances, as we interpret and understand the communications from Spirit. We come to trust the guidance we are given.

Each individual's path is unique. We each must find a balancing method or approach that works for us. Many people remain skeptical about spiritual and psychic abilities until they have an experience that convinces them of the truth. Reading another person's account is no substitute for having your own experience.

Diminishing the power and influence of the ego requires turning within to find the answers to life's questions from our Divine Source. You stop trying to figure everything out with your intellect and, instead, learn to trust your intuition.

DARK NIGHT OF THE SOUL

A crisis often causes us to change our priorities. Facing the *dark night of the soul* or *spiritual emergency*, we shift our attention to focus on the immediate situation.

Perhaps you are overcome with grief following the death of a loved one or feel terrified following the diagnosis of a life-threatening illness. Maybe you have hit bottom after struggling with addiction. You might be going through a divorce, or perhaps you fail to find employment. When you see no way out of your situation, you are willing to listen to divine guidance, the silent voice within. In time, you may see that the crisis served an important purpose.

Saint John of the Cross[3] described this experience a little over four hundred and fifty years ago in his book, *The Dark Night of the Soul*. In essence, he said that we can form a bond with God that will last a lifetime by getting beyond ego and intellect and working directly with soul and Spirit. (This subduing of the ego is sometimes called a shamanic death.)

In these bottoming-out experiences, we are unable to overcome the challenges they bring by ourselves. We have no choice but to turn to a higher power. As we ask the Divine to intervene, we open a new line of communication. The connection we establish can continue for the rest of our lives, as we develop our new relationship with the Divine. Reacting with resistance and anger will not open this channel of communication with God and the opportunity will be lost.

---

[3] In Spanish, San Juan de la Cruz.

THE AUTUMN OF LIFE

In our retirement years, we have the time to teach others and to meditate more. Often, our thoughts move to the end of life as we contemplate our beliefs and reaffirm our deepest convictions. When our attention shifts away from the mundane world, we begin letting go of our homes, careers, hobbies, special interests, and relationships.

Spiritual development never ends; it is a lifetime pursuit. At the age of one hundred, my father relinquished his farm and personal possessions. He moved to a retirement home, where he spent his time studying psychology.

For most of his life, my father was a fatalist about the afterlife. He believed that life ends when the physical body dies. In his final years, though, he began seeing and speaking to his deceased family members. He was preparing for his transition.

Since his passing, we communicate frequently. One morning, over breakfast, I asked for his advice during a time when I was experiencing difficult emotions. He answered in his familiar voice, as a farmer would answer. His advice was to go to the milk barn and milk. I understood the message to focus on my work and remain productive and not be confused by emotional issues that would soon pass. I was happy for his advice and I trust he was happy to be helpful. We continue to communicate regularly.

Beliefs lose their importance as we connect with Source and are guided by Spirit. Developing a personal connection with God helps us become more attuned to the spiritual encounters in our lives. We can easily underestimate how much these experiences influence our decisions and actions, but through study, meditation, and the development of our spiritual gifts we acquire a deeper understanding of the spirit realm. We let go of false beliefs as our connection to the unseen world grows stronger.

CHAPTER 4

FINDING THE LIGHT

" Let there be Light," God said, "and there was Light." The first book of the Bible begins with Genesis, the story of creation. In the Garden of Eden, man was in paradise; he was aware of the spirit realm. But after Adam and Eve ate from the tree of knowledge of good and evil, they no longer had complete access to the spirit realm. Humans became aware of good and evil, of duality, and lost the innocent oneness they'd had in paradise. In order to return to unity consciousness, we must transcend duality and reconnect with the spirit realm.

It is through our experience of duality, however, that we come to a realization of oneness. "Good" and "bad" are judgments we make based on our limited perceptions. When we reach a higher level of understanding, we realize: it's all good.

This understanding develops when our consciousness expands from a lower vibration to a higher vibration. As we vibrate at a higher frequency, we perceive information from higher spiritual realms. Personal effort is necessary to attain higher consciousness. (You cannot simply choose to be more aware. Awareness develops through a process of internal transformation.) Commitment and perseverance are required to overcome dysfunctional patterns and to obtain wisdom.

As you progress along your spiritual path, you may discover a deeper understanding of familiar religious teachings. Your search for meaning may lead you to esoteric teachings. Spiritual encounters can be better understood with a deeper knowledge of the workings of Spirit. A goal worthy of achievement is the mystic marriage, the union of love and wisdom.

Different religions and philosophies present spiritual ideas in different ways. Learning only one tradition may not be enough for you to understand key concepts. You may want to explore multiple traditions. Keep an open mind. One approach may speak to you more than others — and it may not be the tradition within which you were raised. Best to know a little about everything and a lot about something, I always say.

Below I discuss some of the techniques that can be helpful in facilitating spiritual experiences that can help you find the Light. Focus on developing a personal connection with God and awakening consciousness of the spirit realm.

RITUAL, DANCE, AND MOVEMENT

For some people, meditation takes the form of activity. A type of inner silence can be experienced in performance. Dance is a great form of meditation. Also, in athletics, we find that our actions (the performance) and our self (the performer) cannot be separated. Seconds of time seem much longer to the performer while attempting a difficult feat. A hunter sees the buck, turns to shoot, and realizes he pulled the trigger without consciously aiming. The consciousness of the hunter and his action occur simultaneously, without thought.

Ritual, chant, and dance can be used as tools to clear the mind. Dancing all day brings the mind into the present moment. By practicing dance, I developed the ability to meditate any time of the day or night. With a mental command, my mind will go totally quiet.

Just as dance can help us become receptive to our inner world, other physical activities can also shift our awareness. Runners have an open and uncluttered mind that is more receptive to higher guidance. While in "the zone," a runner's awareness is heightened. This heightened state facilitates communication from within.

A sense of awe or numinous feeling may arise when we enter a sacred space (such as a cathedral or temple). Sacred ritual is found in the Catholic Mass, and ecstatic dance is used in Jewish and Sufi traditions. Chanting and ritual are integral parts of Buddhist traditions. (Sufi whirling dervishes, Jewish folk dancers, and Native American dancers all use dance as a ritual practice.)

For centuries, prayer has been an important aspect of church ritual and spiritual practice. As we contemplate, pray, or speak, our thoughts become energized thought forms. Prayer as a spiritual practice can positively influence our lives.

HEIGHTENED AWARENESS

When the United States was engaged in the Desert Storm conflict, I had a premonition during a meditation of two men trying to blow up Air Force fuel tanks. As a former military intelligence officer, I felt compelled to report my experience to the Air Force as a precaution. I contacted the Air Force intelligence service at Tinker Field in Midwest City, Oklahoma. I later read in the newspaper that two men had been arrested for activities which were deemed a threat to the Air Force. I don't know if these two events had any connection, but the fact that I discovered the item in the newspaper seemed to confirm that I had tuned in to something significant as it was occurring.

AWAKENING SPIRITUAL CONSCIOUSNESS

When our awareness expands, we can hear the voice within. The voice speaks guidance and wisdom into our hearts. With greater understanding, we are better able to stop reacting to life's circumstances and, instead, respond in thoughtful, intelligent, positive ways.

Awakening often begins with questioning our beliefs. The search for meaning enriches our lives. Seeing with new eyes and hearing with new ears, we develop spiritual senses that can help us discern the truth. (The ultimate decision maker on truth is your higher self. You instinctively know what rings true when you pay attention to your inner guidance.)

Awakening spiritual consciousness can induce joy and euphoria, yet more personal work must be done in order to have spiritual experiences on a continuous basis. Through acquiring wisdom, we develop good judgment and integrity, and love becomes ever more present in our lives.

CHAPTER 5

OUR ENERGY BODIES

M ultiple bodies, visible and invisible, make up our being. We recognize our normal five physical senses in their regular and practical use. Less recognized are our heightened or spiritual senses. These senses become more available to us through development of psychic perception and awareness.

SPIRITUAL SENSES

Just as we have physical senses, we have corresponding spiritual senses. These expanded senses are more developed in some people, just as vision and hearing can vary from one person to another. *Clairvoyance* is the ability to gain information through extrasensory perception and can be thought of as advanced sight. Being farsighted or having great insight and "vision" are aspects of this heightened sense.

Clairaudience is hearing the voice of Spirit and is another heightened sense. Hearing with the inner ear is advanced hearing and may manifest as telepathic messaging.

Clairsentience is the ability to feel the past, present, and future physical and emotional states of others through sensing their subtle energies with our higher senses. A clairsentient can retrieve information from houses or public buildings or by holding an object that belonged to someone. *(Psychometry* is the ability to gain impressions from an object by extrasensory perception.) A photograph can sometimes reveal a person's emotional disposition to a clairsentient individual.

We each have other spiritual senses, too, including the senses of smell and taste. Our olfactory senses might detect specific odors or fragrances that are present for no earthly reason. These may be coming from the invisible planes. (Someone might suddenly smell a departed grandmother's perfume, for example, and realize that she is present in spirit.)

An olfactory psychic experience happened to me while I was working in my mid-town office, which is decorated with original Native American paintings. I was in the copy room when I smelled a strong odor of sage. Usually when there is no known cause, an odor indicates that someone is present in spirit. The scent of sage suggested the presence of a Native American medicine man in spirit. I did not hear any messages or voices; I was simply aware of his presence. I often sense my mother and father in spirit, and I am aware that my spirit teachers are always near, but it was unusual for me to sense the presence of a spiritual entity other than my teachers and ancestors.

Taste can be described as an appreciation of beauty and aesthetics.

The mystical sense of *claircognizance* (often referred to as our "sixth sense") is the ability to receive knowledge intuitively. (We don't know how we know, we just know.)

PRANA

The universal energy responsible for our bodily functions is called *prana* (in *Sanskrit)* or chi (in Chinese). Prana flows through, within, and around us at all times. Prana comprises all cosmic energy, permeating the universe on all levels. This energy sustains life and animates our physical form. In all living beings, prana is drawn in through the breath.

OUR INVISIBLE BODIES

Surrounding each of us is an electromagnetic field known as an aura. This subtle substance consists of several layers (sometimes called "bodies"). These layers include the physical body, an etheric body, an astral body, a mental body, and the spiritual bodies. These invisible bodies may be listed or illustrated in a way that suggests they are in distinct sequential layers, but they occupy interchangeable space and may overlap and intermingle. They are distinguished by their rates of vibration.

We are born with these bodies. (We bring them with us from our previous life incarnation.) They extend beyond the visible body and make up the auric envelope or *auric egg.* The auric egg does not disintegrate upon death; it continues throughout our many lifetimes.

The etheric body, which is located about an inch from the physical body, is the name given in *Neo-Theosophy* to the layer that is closest to the physical body. The etheric body interacts with the chemical and electrical parts of the physical body.

The astral body is the gateway to the *psyche*. It is the unconscious storehouse of our habits and emotions.

The mental body stores information it receives from our perceptions and experiences. It also transmits this information to the causal body, one of our spiritual bodies. (Information about the spiritual bodies is presented in Chapter 11.)

The ongoing interplay between these different bodies affects one's overall life experience for better or for worse. For example, unhealthy mental patterns can express in the physical body as disease.[4] When we feel sad, perhaps after experiencing a loss or disappointment, we weep, expressing our sadness through a physical response. (We may also cry when we experience physical pain.) As your mind registers the gravity of a situation, your emotions are activated. A wave of peace may come upon you when you feel the presence of Spirit, or you may feel a tingle down your spine. A psychic impression may register as a gut feeling. When you receive an important message from your inner voice, you may feel awe and appreciation, and respond emotionally with exhilaration.

---

[4] See Louise Hay's book *Heal Your Body: The Mental Causes for Physical Illness and the Metaphysical Way to Overcome Them* for a list of various ailments and the mental causes and remedies that she discovered intuitively.

The auric egg is often depicted in religious art (in the Christian tradition, at least) with a halo or *aureola* around the heads of holy figures, such as Jesus, Mary, and the saints. The golden aura around spiritually evolved religious figures signifies their holiness.

In different phases of life, our focus changes. The aura reflects these changes. (During the time that I was pursuing wisdom studies, my aura was white. As I changed my focus to teaching, my aura turned green.)

A person of high intellect may have a lot of yellow in her aura. As she transitions from intellectual pursuits to a more devotional or spiritual focus, her aura may reflect yellow (intellect) as well as purple (devotion).

The color red may predominate while a person is experiencing an intense emotion such as anger, whereas an orange color represents the vibrancy of the life force. If your aura is predominantly one color, but has a little red, you may still be processing some incident that made you angry. Having several colors in your aura is common and indicates that several parts of your being are actively engaged.

We are sending and receiving information all the time through psychic communication. Upon meeting someone for the first time, your initial response may be positive or negative as you sense that person's energy field. By touching someone, you may receive an impression about his temperament.

Every thought generates a vibration in the mental body. The thought assumes a floating form, and the color reflects the nature and intensity of the thought. The thought forms in a person who is depressed may appear as gray to a clairvoyant. (When a person suffers from severe clinical depression, the negative thought forms can appear almost black.) Thoughts are things; they have power and influence in our lives. To change our lives, we must change our thoughts.

Many traditions recognize the validity of hands-on healing. We can use the energy that flows from our hands to heal ourselves and others. Visualize holding your hands with the palms together, then feel the energy moving between your palms as you move your hands closer together or farther apart. The energy you are feeling radiates outward and has healing qualities. Reiki is one practice that uses the hands for healing.

As we learn about our energy bodies, we become aware of how we interact with others and with the world. We gain an understanding of our perceptions and gifts. We see that we are more than just mind and body; each of us is a complex interactive system of bodies that record, store, and retrieve thoughts and emotions. We are integrated spiritual beings.

Discernment is required when using spiritual gifts, for, if misused they can be harmful.

CHAPTER 6

SPIRITUAL ABUSE AND ABUSE OF SPIRITUAL GIFTS

Abuse of spiritual gifts occurs anytime someone uses spiritual knowledge or gifts in a way that is detrimental to others. Spiritual abuse occurs when religious leaders misuse their positions and cause trauma in their followers, whether or not they intend to cause harm. Spiritual leaders must be willing to acknowledge their own shortcomings and guard against judging those with less awareness.

Some religions profess that their way is the only way to Heaven. Heaven must be a lonely place if it is only occupied by their members! By dominating his congregation, a religious leader, whether a pastor or a priest, may instill fear, guilt, or other negative emotions instead of love and trust. He may seek obedience rather than fellowship and caution his followers against listening to the voice of "the devil." This tactic is designed to keep members dependent on church leaders for spiritual guidance.

However, we are all spiritual beings, and, as such, we must stay open to inner guidance — our personal communication with God. *Do not give your power away when religious or, in some cultures, governmental authorities try to control your thoughts and behavior.* Even if you are forced to take part in church ceremonies and activities, your search for truth can remain strong until you are able to remove yourself from what may be a dysfunctional or toxic situation. Take a break, change the setting, find a safer place to practice your faith. Many churches offer a trusting, accepting experience and follow the principles taught by Jesus, Buddha, or another master.

Inappropriate physical touching and sexual exploitation by spiritual leaders is clearly abusive and is too often tolerated within church organizations. Harassment, intimidation, or requests for sexual favors are all forms of abuse and can damage the psyche. Violating a child is a crime. When someone's heart *chakra* is fully open, he would never knowingly harm another. Honor your own awareness and feelings in all situations.

Be wary of advertisements claiming to help you achieve higher consciousness by attending a weekend workshop. If a program sounds too good to be true, it may be a scam. A teacher may provide guidance or pointers for personal work, but spiritual growth takes many years of dedicated effort. Is the teacher who is offering the pointers living an advanced spiritual life herself? Does he practice humility, reverence, and gratitude, or is he more interested in fame and fortune? A person teaching prosperity while living in abject poverty may not have much to teach you! Don't be afraid to ask about a person's qualifications and experience if you have doubts about his or her authenticity and integrity.

Certain disingenuous psychics or charlatans want access to your bank account. For only a few thousand dollars, they'll promise to help you get that new car or find your soul mate. This practice is unethical and violates the trust you put in them when you seek their help. Genuine intuitive mediums will give you an unbiased message with no personal interpretation at a fair price. Authentic teachers do not seek personal gain, nor will they simply tell you what they think you want to hear. They do not try to cultivate dependency but offer their gifts in service to your growth and development.

Unwisely invoking spiritual forces can be dangerous if you do not know what you are doing. The Kabbalah, for example, includes stories about people that go insane, commit suicide, or suffer other harms when attempting to awaken their spiritual bodies without guidance, protection, or readiness. Table tipping or lifting a table in a circle may be fun and exciting, but these kinds of activities can be dangerous because they invoke the elementals, a class of beings below the human race in consciousness. Elementals will cooperate — sometimes — but they can be mischievous and do not always work in a way that benefits humans.

I learned this lesson the hard way when I decided to try dowsing with a pendulum. I failed to invoke spiritual protection (i.e., asking my teachers, masters, and angels to protect me and surrounding myself with white light). Unknowingly, I opened a portal in my psyche and allowed entities to enter into my mind. I heard voices for a few years before I straightened myself back out. I have stayed away from dowsing since that experience. I find it is safer and more reliable to ask and get the answer directly.

Black magic is the use of dark forces and should be avoided, as it can have dangerous consequences. When you give up your free will to a dark entity, you are allowing that entity into your psyche. This intrusion can lead to an obsession in your mind and, in extreme cases, possession. (Possession occurs when an entity overcomes your free will. A helpful book about this subject is *Obsession and Possession* by Torkom Saraydarian.)

White magic is always based on love, not control or manipulation. (Prayer work, for example, is a form of white magic.) Spiritual development may enable us to use some of the occult laws for the accomplishment of positive results.

When seeking a spiritual teacher or guide, look for those individuals who promote healthy and constructive interaction. Likewise, in developing your own spiritual gifts, you must remain vigilant to ensure that you use them wisely and avoid causing harm.

Spirit Shield Mandala

SPIRIT SHIELD MANDALA

I chose this acrylic painting by Erwin Newton from my personal collection for contemplation as a mandala. "Spirit Shield" is an automatic painting, made by the artist while contemplating shamanism after the artist lost his brother. I saw this painting five or six years before the artist was ready to sell it, and I was grateful to eventually own it. I often visualize a spirit shield in front of me when I am navigating a crowd of people to keep my aura clear of outside influences.

Meditate and focus on this image and decide what the image means to you.

What do you see? Perhaps you will see a spirit shield, as I do.

ABOUT THE ARTIST

Erwin Newton

Erwin studied at the Art Institute in Chicago from 2000 until 2005. There, he was exposed to like-minded artists and professors. His study of poetry and music influences the mood of his paintings. By keeping his mind distracted, he creates universes not seen, the world inside his head. Using pen and ink, he first sketches his renditions.

Erwin now paints and creates in his studio in Belen, New Mexico. Inspired by his surroundings — sky, mountains, animals and birds and objects — he sees patterns and textures in nature that influence his work. He said:

> Painting is a release of anxiety and stress and calms me. My paintings are unconscious expressions of spiritual consciousness. Surrealism is my greatest influence. Abstract expressionism and aboriginal art, especially the oceanic art, inspires my work.
>
> — Erwin Newton

CHAPTER 7

A SHAMANIC CRISIS

Our greatest gift sometimes comes from overcoming our greatest challenge. Those who are ready for a great undertaking will be tested. Many people experience a "midlife crisis," but mine was a spiritual emergency. Having psychic perception throughout my life did not prepare me for the turmoil I felt. My very foundation was shaken. I was overcome with despair. A form of madness ensued, and I was tormented by voices. The auditory hallucinations caused tremendous disruption in my life. The recovery process required years of integration and searching for meaning before I reached a point of feeling comfortable in my skin again.

I was living in Houston when the voices started. I was in my early forties, and the episodes were so disruptive that I quit work, moved my possessions into storage, and lived for over a year with no income and no stable residence. I felt a devastating loss of control, and real terror.

In addition to hearing voices, I felt a crawling sensation in my body that I can only describe as snakelike. What I did not realize at the time was that, as a result of my spiritual work, the *kundalini* had awakened and was moving up my spine, through my chakras. (Kundalini is a form of primal energy that remains dormant at the base of the spine until it is awakened. The rising of the kundalini is often compared to a coiled snake unwinding.)

A snake's skin doesn't grow; it stretches. When it can stretch no more, the snake sheds its skin and grows a new one. The snake, therefore, symbolizes the sloughing off of the trappings of an old life, as we too must allow restrictive, outmoded ways of being to be sloughed off so we can continue to grow.

I suffered hallucinations from 1992 until 1995. In addition to hearing voices, I saw apparitions. My friends and family were very worried about me during this period. My family helped all they could and were very patient and understanding, but I lost many friends, as my former friends had no role in the new life I was entering. I had begun a journey into unfamiliar territory. I often asked myself if I was insane, as my life seemed unreal.

Many stories from ancient literature tell of a hero being exiled, going on a journey, and returning home after trials. I wandered around Texas and Oklahoma seeking help from family, friends, and professionals. I felt like the Fool depicted in the *Tarot* card deck. I was lost in a void and seemed to be roaming, but I was seeking a return to health, where work and self-sufficiency were possible.

To attain a deeper and expanded level of consciousness, a transformation is necessary. The transformation process feels like death. When a person experiences a psychological death, but does not physically die, his consciousness perceives God in a new way. His whole physical, mental, emotional, and spiritual being is penetrated by a new energy. Transcendence of the ego is necessary in order to unite with the Divine Spirit within.

By 1995, I had spent twenty years reading Manly P. Hall's books. Steeped in a philosophical system, I was better able to interpret my kundalini/shamanic experience, but spiritual pride was impeding my progress.

The spiritual emergency humbled me. I realized I did not know everything. The false personality or ego mask I had erected fell away. My spiritual awareness expanded to a new level of understanding, and I was able to overcome the spiritual pride that I had been feeling.

I was having trouble functioning in a normal way, yet, on a deep level, I did not feel fear. My early connection with God and the universe gave me an unshakable faith. Therefore, I believed that everything would turn out okay.

I saw my first apparition while I was at my brother's house watching a conference on television one evening. Political leaders from Israel and Palestine were speaking from a podium. I saw Reptilians standing behind some of them, overshadowing them. (Reptilians are beings that reside on the astral plane. They are not human. They have a warring nature and try to influence human activities.)

I found the experience distressing and consulted with

several psychiatrists. One suggested that I was having a panic attack, another thought I was suffering from schizophrenia, and a third said I had a chemical imbalance in my brain. None of these professionals recognized that I was having a spiritual crisis. My father, who liked to read about psychology, believed my symptoms were caused by overwhelming stress in my life.

I believe I was experiencing a breakdown of my personality. I adopted a simplified lifestyle, living in isolation, keeping a low profile, and feeling a lot of humility, gratitude, and compassion for others. I began to understand the stories of the Bible as metaphors for the awakening process rather than as historical events.

As I returned to normal functioning, I began hearing a voice from Spirit. This voice was logical and rational, and it was saying, "Go see your son, he is going to be a father." This message repeated over several days. I had lost track of where my son was, so I went to the courthouse and asked to see a record of my child support payments. The report showed the address of my ex-wife.

Following the guidance of Spirit, I went to find my seventeen-year-old son. I brought along a print of a painting depicting a father holding an infant to give to him. I found the house and knocked on the door. My son answered and said, "Hello Dad. I am going to be a father." Despite my efforts to stay in contact, he has chosen not to include me in his life, but from a metaphysical point of view, the birth of my first grandchild paralleled the new birth occurring within me.

After about nine years of living in a secluded state and keeping a low profile, I felt a sense of completion and knew that I could enter the world again. Healed and ready for a new beginning, I moved to Tulsa, Oklahoma in September 2003 to be closer to two of my brothers. In Tulsa, I began attending the Unity Center of Tulsa and the Church of Religious Science (which is now called the Center for Spiritual Living) to meet other like-minded people. I co-founded a local metaphysical church (the Center of Light) and began teaching.

I was also drawn to *shamanism* and read several books, including *Shamanic Spirit* by Kenneth Meadows. Listening to the drumming compact disc that came with the book, I was able to enter a trance state. I asked Spirit about the success of my new accounting practice. When I returned to conscious awareness, I saw a vision of the Venus of Willendorf and felt awed by the abundance of nature. This vision gave me a connection with fertility, the Divine Feminine, and Mother Earth for the first time, as I felt my heart chakra open.

Later, after losing a client, I decided to use the shamanic trance method to seek information. This time, when I returned to conscious awareness I envisioned a chalice filled with water, but the chalice overturned and the water poured out. I felt upset, until I was shown a large pitcher filled with water, from which the chalice could be refilled many times. God's abundance is unlimited.

When I told a shaman friend in New Mexico about my psychotic experiences nearly twenty years earlier, he said I was describing the classic shamanic initiation and referred me to the book *Shamanism: Archaic Techniques of Ecstasy.* Reading about the shamanic madness experienced by tribal members selected to become shamans, I felt reassured about my initiation experience

Pride may not be an obstacle in your life that keeps you from advancing on your spiritual path; perhaps it is fear or greed or guilt. Your willingness to face whatever demons confront you on your own journey to wholeness will determine the degree of understanding you are able to achieve.

I am grateful for the psychological and spiritual healing I experienced. I emerged humble, strong, determined, and productive. I have a lovely wife, a beautiful home, a lake house, family relationships, an active accounting practice, and many friends. Life is good.

CHAPTER 8

SPIRIT GUIDES

My guides and spirit teachers have been visiting me since childhood, usually when I'm asleep. Over the years, I have become more aware of the communication as my perception has increased. Developing a relationship with my spirit teachers only occurred after much spiritual study and personal development. My spirit teachers have been working with me in earnest since I began studying the ancient *esoteric* wisdom.

I am not clairvoyant, however, and I do not ordinarily see visions or hear voices (I receive telepathic messages), so I sometimes seek the aid of an intuitive reader named Bright Eyes to provide a more complete understanding of my spirit teachers' messages, which are often visual images. Bright Eyes receives information about me from the unseen world. (My spirit teachers reveal visual pictures and symbols to her, and she shares the information with me.) With each new revelation, my relationship with my spirit teachers becomes stronger.

During a soul reading, Bright Eyes will look at my physical, emotional, mental, and spiritual health and tell me what she sees or hears about each area. Sometimes a discarnate being, such as my spirit teacher, provides wisdom and guidance. During one reading, Bright Eyes described what she saw as an owl in the front of a classroom, teaching. The owl was wearing a mortarboard with a golden tassel and a gown. To me, the owl represents magic and mystery.

In my younger days, the only spiritual book I knew was the Bible and I was eager to learn all I could from its mysteries. Even then, I believed the Bible could be read allegorically and not everything in it is to be taken literally. I wanted to understand the symbolic meaning and to discover the truth hidden within the text and stories.

At age twenty-five, I joined the Masonic Order and ultimately became a thirty-second degree Freemason. (The thirty-third degree is an honorary degree bestowed after a lifetime of contributions to society. Manly P. Hall was awarded the thirty-third degree in 1973.)

In the late 1980s, I discovered the Chapel of Light in Lake Whitney, Texas. There, I met an intuitive artist, Elaine, who was offering colored pencil drawings of people's spirit guides. I paid for a pencil drawing and Elaine drew a picture of five of my spirit guides. She explained that my spirit teachers work with me at night while I sleep. Having a picture helped me visualize them.

About fifteen years later, my intuitive friend Lorraine gave me the names of my spirit guides. She told me that my primary teacher is Josephus. Lorraine saw that he wore a beard and dressed in a robe similar to the ones worn at the time of Jesus. With this information, I was able to identify each of my five spirit teachers. Josephus is the primary spokesman for all of them.

In 2005, I had a session with Bright Eyes, who also had studied Manly P. Hall's writings. She said Josephus was present and he gave her a message that it was time for me to start teaching. As I had spent most of my life studying the mysteries, I accepted that I was ready to share what I had learned. I began to teach spiritual subjects in New Thought churches in Tulsa.

The following year, Josephus was again present during a reading with Bright Eyes. He showed her an image of me standing with him in robes, and he gave her the message that I was graduating. This gave me a great feeling of accomplishment, as I had studied on my own for many years. In another reading, Bright Eyes told me she saw Josephus sitting on a throne, as *Hierophant*, and I was kneeling before him with my head bowed. He placed a crown on my head. After receiving these messages, I felt confident that I was ready to teach what I had learned about the ancient mysteries.[5]

---

[5] Later, I found information about the degrees of initiation in the mystery schools in the book *The Mystery Schools* by Grace Knoche, a former leader of the Theosophical Society. According to Knoche, as a person advances in understanding, he reaches a point of experience and knowledge that qualifies him to teach the mysteries.

Developing higher consciousness is a lifetime endeavor. My spirit teacher Josephus has overseen my progress in the study of the ancient wisdom and the world's religions. My lifelong passion for learning has resulted in the accumulation of over 2,000 volumes of spiritual and esoteric literature, including the writings of the Rosicrucians, the Theosophists, the Anthroposophists, Manly P. Hall, and many others.

My home has become a sanctuary where I study, and I also teach the mysteries to individuals who have an interest. My students have told me that my work with them changed their lives for the better. This positive feedback helps sustain me in my efforts to teach anyone who is interested in learning.

My spirit teachers continue to work with me and through me. Josephus and I communicate on a regular basis. In 2007, I saw an apparition of another of my spirit guides, Gabriella, in my den. Her loving presence affirmed the changes I've made to bring beauty into my home and to make it a sanctuary.

Several years later, I received a telepathic message that I would find a painting to go above one of my bookcases, so I kept an observant eye for several years. Then I found a picture in a book of the fifteenth-century painting by Tang Yin of China, "The Thatched Hut of Dreaming of an Immortal," which hangs in one of the Smithsonian Institution's Asian art museums. The painting depicts a man meditating in a thatched cottage, but his spirit is shown floating in the sky above mountains. I felt this was the perfect painting for my bedroom, so I ordered a print of the painting from an art gallery and placed it above the bookcase in my bedroom. There, it reminds me that each night when I sleep, I travel the astral plane to meet with my spirit teacher, Josephus.

Meditation is the most effective method I have found for getting telepathic messages from spirit guides and teachers. Ask and you shall receive. The messages I receive help me write lessons for the classes I teach and guided me in writing this book. With the continuing communication from my spirit teachers, I feel that I am walking with them and in step with their guidance every day.

CHAPTER 9

THE FOURTH
NOBLE TRUTH:
THE EIGHTFOLD PATH

I n the first sermon he gave after his enlightenment, Buddha delivered the Four Noble Truths, which became the foundation of Buddhism. Simply stated, they are:

1. The truth of suffering (*dukkha*)
2. The truth of the cause of suffering
3. The truth of the cure for suffering
4. The truth of the path leading to the cessation of suffering (The Eightfold Path)

The human experience involves suffering. Everything on this plane of existence is impermanent, even joy. The Eightfold Path is designed to help us overcome suffering.

Following the Eightfold Path can lead a seeker to enlightenment. The Path shows a way to live in harmony with all creation. The Path leads one to balance, equilibrium, and a feeling of equanimity. As we develop compassion, loving-kindness, and wisdom, this practice becomes a way of living. (Buddhist practices can be used by anyone.) People sometimes embrace these practices when they realize that they can no longer drift aimlessly through life.

RIGHT VIEW/RIGHT UNDERSTANDING

The first step on the Path is *right view* or right understanding. This step comes at the beginning of the Path and again at the end of the Path, for the steps are not actually sequential even though we speak of them as if they were. When we adopt a right view, we are steered toward right action and eventually attain freedom from suffering. We become gentle-minded, peaceful, loving, and courageous.

In order to hold the right view, we must purge our minds of false ideas. One way to do that is through the study of wisdom teachings, which provide a framework for our attitudes and actions. When we know truth, we do not need to believe or accept the views of others as a matter of faith.

RIGHT INTENTION/RIGHT THOUGHT

The second step on the Eightfold Path is *right intention* or right thinking. Right thinking follows right understanding. Our thoughts are things and influence who we become and what we manifest. When we approach people and situations with a set of preconceived ideas, we are unable to see things as they really are. Right thinking teaches us to view situations with a calm mind that is present in the moment. We are able to see clearly because we are not carrying the baggage of the past or projecting into the future.

According to Buddhist teachings, there are two kinds of thoughts: wandering thoughts and logical, directed thoughts. The untrained mind moves in a scattered, haphazard manner, rushing from idea to idea. When our thoughts wander, we have little control over them.

When trained, the mind remains focused on its object without wavering. When we are focused on a task, our thoughts are directed; our will takes hold and directs our intentions in a particular direction. Practicing right thinking and right intention requires renouncing desire and developing good will and harmlessness.

By being mindful of our thoughts and feelings, we can experience the happiness and joy that come from having a heart filled with loving-kindness and compassion. You can begin with feeling compassion and loving-kindness towards yourself. Further into your practice, you are better able to extend compassion and loving-kindness towards all sentient beings.

RIGHT SPEECH

The effects of speech are not immediate and can easily be overlooked. Our words carry a vibration. Others feel the vibration of our voice in their bodies and with their senses. When speech originates from friendship and harmony, it conveys loving-kindness and sympathy.

With the third step, *right speech*, we begin the practice of moral discipline and ethical conduct. Our speech must be truthful and not cause disharmony. It must not include lies, exaggeration, insults, or hypocrisy. Idle chatter is pointless and lacks purpose or depth. Truthful speech is an expression of our wisdom and understanding.

Right speech requires abstaining from false speech, slanderous speech, harsh speech, and gossip. Right speech is like a treasure; it is uttered at the right moment, moderate, and full of sense. Right speech acknowledges the oneness of all things and brings harmony, not strife.

There is a saying that if we do not have anything good to say then it is best to remain silent. Sometimes we must speak out against wrongdoing, out of righteous judgment, but this kind of action results from the wisdom that accompanies a loving heart.

RIGHT ACTION

Right action means we act without selfish attachment to our work or to the outcome of our acts. We act mindfully, without causing discord. Right action springs from compassion and from an understanding of *dharma,* a way of living that expresses loving-kindness, wisdom, quiescence, generosity, and virtue.

When we adopt the principle of right action, we do not engage in actions that are contrary to right thinking and right understanding. We refrain from lying, stealing, misusing sex, and abusing or harming others. Compassion is not a passive state — it is active. It is a choice. When we act with wisdom and compassion, harmonious results follow. Right action flows from knowing when to act and when to be still, when to work in the outer realms and when to work in the inner realms.

RIGHT LIVELIHOOD

Right livelihood, the next step on the Path, includes doing wholesome work that does not cause injury to other sentient beings. Right livelihood means that one earns a living in a righteous way — peacefully, honestly, and morally. Right livelihood includes holding the intention to help others work and to be a benefit to society. When you know why you are here, you are better able to express your life purpose through your livelihood. You align your chosen occupation, your purpose, and your values. Training and refinement lead to becoming a master of your craft and allow you greater self-expression.

RIGHT EFFORT

The sixth step, *right effort*, includes withdrawing attention from unwholesome thoughts that arise in us. This practice leads to serenity and insight. We must refrain from frivolous pursuits and mindless activities that dissipate our energy. Right effort requires diligence, exertion, and perseverance. Through right effort we cultivate wholesome states of mind. Maintaining wholesome states of mind can lead to rapture and bliss. As our subconscious mind becomes filled with compassion and loving- kindness, right effort becomes a habit and is reflected in our actions.

RIGHT MINDFULNESS

Step seven is *right mindfulness*, which requires awakened attention — being awake and aware and living as a conscious being. We must release habits that maintain the illusion of a separate self. Being nonjudgmental, we clearly see things the way they are. Our views are not distorted by opinions and preferences.

Mindfulness applies to more than our minds. We become aware of our physical bodies, our feelings, and our mental states. For example, in meditation we can observe when sensations arise and when they go.

Mindfulness is a presence of mind — attentiveness or awareness that allows deep concentration. Mindfulness is part of the path to purity and to overcoming suffering.

In Buddhist teachings, the four immeasurables — loving-kindness, compassion, empathic joy, and equanimity — occur naturally with the practice of right mindfulness and meditation. Feeling bliss during meditation is common. The welfare of others must be centermost in our minds in this practice.

Right Concentration

The eighth and final step is *right concentration*. Right concentration hones our mental faculties, which are necessary in every state of consciousness. Right concentration leads to insight and wisdom. In my meditation, I go beyond mind to reach the spirit realm, where I am able to communicate with my spirit teachers. *Paranormal* perception is common in a state of deep concentration and contemplation.

Most people experience life as suffering. The Eightfold Path provides the basis for overcoming suffering, mental afflictions, and destructive emotions. The continued practice of meditation, mindfulness, and concentration along with contemplation leads to a breakthrough in consciousness and development of compassion and loving-kindness.

These eight steps are not separate; they are intertwined. We practice them all simultaneously. Meditation can help us see clearly and achieve mental stability. As we experience pain and overcome adversity, we gain greater compassion for others who suffer.

I have been following the Eightfold Path for many years. These practices have helped me find my spiritual center and understand my inner perceptions. I am reminded to be aware of my every thought, intention, and action.

CHAPTER 10

SILENCE: BEYOND BRAIN CHATTER

S ilence is difficult to find in our modern world, but through various meditation practices we can achieve a state of inner quiet, even in a noisy environment. Silence provides a space beyond thoughts to achieve clarity. Realization occurs more quickly when a seeker learns to reach a state of *No Mind*.

Various techniques for discovering silence have existed since time immemorial. One method involves substituting a positive thought for a negative thought. This is a good practice to follow — in life as well as in meditation. We learn to assume the position of witness, watching our thoughts come and go without giving them attention or analysis. When the ego/mind releases its thoughts, the mind enters a period of quiet.

Visualizing a painting or inspiring image helps to calm and quiet the mind and to reduce brain chatter so that a state of complete awareness can be attained. (Following your breath can have a similar effect.) It is in this state of silence that one can hear the voice of God.

Many religious traditions incorporate a practice like meditation or contemplation as a means of communing with the Divine. (Some monastic orders require a vow of silence.) In our heart of hearts, we know God is silence.

> Osho's writings differentiate between silence and noiselessness:

> Silence usually is understood to be something negative, something empty, an absence of sound, of noises. This misunderstanding is prevalent because very few people have ever experienced silence. All that they have experienced in the name of silence is noiselessness. But silence is a totally different phenomenon. It is utterly positive. It is existential, it is not empty. It is overflowing with a music that you have never heard before, with a fragrance that is unfamiliar to you, with a light that can only be seen by the inner eyes.[6]

---

[6] Osho, *Meditation: The First and Last Freedom* (New York: St. Martin's Press, 1996), 6.

Osho notes that truth is found in emptiness. "Truth is attained in silence and lost in speech."[7] God gives us two ears and one mouth. Therefore, we should listen more and talk less. We learn more by listening than by talking in most cases.

Meditation involves listening to the silent voice within. During meditation, you watch your thoughts and let them pass without attaching any emotion to them. In this way, you find tranquility within. You come to know yourself — the advice given in the Greek mystery schools to admonish each of us to access our own inner wisdom, which we interpret to the best of our understanding.

My favorite of Manly P. Hall's writings is *Self-Unfoldment by Disciplines of Realization,* in which Hall instructs how to concentrate:

> Concentration is not essentially an intellectual process. While the mind is the instrument of concentration, the exercises fail if they are regarded as directed toward mental control through effort.

> Concentration involves the simultaneous activity of every part of the consciousness: There must be attention without tension. There must be feeling without emotion; visualization without fixation. And all must be bound together by an

[7] Osho, *The Song of Ecstasy: Talks on Adi Shankara's Bhai Govindam* (Pune, India: Rebel Publishing House, 2000), 4.

inclusive one-pointedness of purpose which does
not include any inference of limitation.[8]

As Hall explains, the process of concentration occurs simultaneously on different planes of consciousness. We come to realize that our feelings and thoughts are connected and that the things sensed are identical with the power to sense. "There is no division in between the flower and its beauty, the bird and its grace, or the river and its song," Hall writes.[9] "Realization brings the Truth to the wise man exactly what the wise man brings to Truth."[10]

A Zen koan states, "We shape clay into a pot, but it is the emptiness inside that holds whatever we want." Likewise, in meditation, you empty your mind by clearing thoughts so that consciousness can fill the space with useful information. Upon quieting your mind, finding inner peace, and awakening your inner ear, you may receive impressions from the unconscious during meditation as you contemplate the silence. You may also be able to hear from your spirit teachers and from Divine Source.

Helena P. Blavatsky also writes about the clay vessel:

---

[8] Manly P. Hall, *Self-Unfoldment by Disciplines of Realization* (1942, repr., Los Angeles: Philosophical Research Society, 1977), 100.
[9] Ibid.
[10] Ibid., 101.

Before the soul can see, the Harmony within must be attained, and fleshly eyes be rendered blind to all illusion.

Before the Soul can hear, the image (man) has to become as deaf to roarings as to whispers, to cries of bellowing elephants as to the silvery buzzing of the golden fire-fly.

Before the soul can comprehend and may remember, she must unto the Silent Speaker be united just as the form to which the clay is modelled, is first united with the potter's mind.

For then the soul will hear, and will remember.

And then to the inner ear will speak —

THE VOICE OF THE SILENCE.[11]

In No Mind you become the observer, conscious of being conscious. Through No Mind and nonaction, you are led by Spirit to the correct action. This is realization through No Mind.

The practice that Unity Worldwide Ministries uses is similar to the Zen practice of No Mind. Unity's publication, *Meditation in the Silence*, describes the discerning power of the intuition.

---

[11] H. P. Blavatsky, trans., *The Voice of the Silence: Being Chosen Fragments from the "Book of the Golden Precepts,"* Blavatsky Centenary Edition (1889; repr., Edmonton, Canada: Edmonton Theosophical Society, 1991), 2–3.

Intuition has its seat in the more sensitive portion
of our sympathetic nervous system, known as
the solar plexus; our spiritual revelations come
through this inner sense, which seems to have its
means of contact with our consciousness in the
very innermost parts of our being. Going within
therefore has a double significance. God is spirit,
and the things of God are spiritually discerned:
that is the revelation sought in the process of
going within, for it is through discernment by
the inner intuitional nature that this revelation
actually comes into consciousness. Silence
therefore is only a means to an end. One must
constantly go beyond the point of mere mental
stillness and allow the elements of the spiritual
realm to come forth into consciousness.[12]

We ordinarily think of nonaction as the opposite of action.
The Chinese *I Ching*, an ancient manual of divination, presents
nonaction as effortless, unselfconscious action.

The precipitating action is achieved through
perseverance: holding firmly inside ourselves to
what is true and correct, yet taking no action;
we allow ourself to be led by the Creative, rather
than by intellectual calculation. When we take

[12] Unity Worldwide Ministries, *Meditation in the Silence* (Kansas City, MO: Unity Books), 38–39.

matters into our hands, because of emotional pressure, we interfere with its beneficial action. Yet by holding firm, by not taking any action urged by our fearful or boastful inferior nature, by clinging to the Creative and its action, we assist in bringing about the correct result. Through non-action — doing nothing at all — we achieve everything.[13]

These various traditions are describing different techniques that can be used to achieve a state of silence or no-thought.

As Manly P. Hall observed, illumination is not a single experience that catapults us from a state of ignorance to a state of wisdom. Rather, it follows a series of spiritual discoveries. Some moments will seem more radiant than others, but illumination occurs over many lifetimes. Growth is a process of unfoldment marked by the gradual increase of internal light.

Illumination always takes the form of solution, solving the problem most imminent to the Self. The composer with his unfinished symphony, the artist with his unfinished canvas, the poet with his unfinished verses, and the scientist with his unfinished experiments – each of these is confronted with a problem; each has gone as far as he can proceed unaided. Having exhausted

---

[13] Carol K. Anthony, *A Guide to the I Ching* (Stow, MA: Anthony Publishing Company, 1982), 1.

the resources of conscious personal knowledge, each is groping for a solution. It may require days, months, or even years to complete the unfinished task. Without a revelation, only some mystical extension of consciousness can make possible the completion of the work.

Then the light comes. How, no man knows; when, no man knows; why, no man knows.[14]

There are many different ways we can practice quieting the mind. Experiment with several and find one that works best for you. Staying with a practice is important to allow the knowledge and wisdom from the invisible world entrance into our consciousness on a regular basis.

---

[14] Ibid., 188.

CHAPTER 11

CONSCIOUSNESS BETWEEN DEATH AND REBIRTH

S ince the earliest civilizations, people have wondered whether death is the end. Different cultures have developed myths about where we came from and where we will go after we die. However, the understanding that consciousness continues after death is older than written records.

A lifetime of communicating with ancestors and spirit guides is evidence enough for me to accept that consciousness extends beyond death. I find in communicating with my deceased dad that he has the same emotional patterns and intellectual abilities that he had in life. He does not appear to have been spirited away to Heaven as he thought he would be.

Some Christians see the afterlife as a period of waiting for the Second Coming, a time of the Last Judgment, when Christ will return to Earth. The Christian idea of Heaven is similar to that region described as the "mind world" by Theosophist Annie Besant in *Man and His Bodies.*

> This third region, that I have called the mind world, includes, though it is not identical with, that which is familiar to the Theosophists under the name of Devachan or Devaloka, the land of the Gods, the happy or blessed land, as some translate it. Devachan bears that name because of its nature and condition, nothing interfering with that world which may cause pain or sorrow; it is a specially guarded state, into which positive evil is not allowed to intrude, the blissful resting-place of man in which he peacefully assimilates the fruits of his physical life.[15]

The Theosophical and Eastern teachings provide an orderly, logical, and compelling explanation of what happens after death. Theosophy derives much of its philosophy from Hinduism. The Hindus have many teachings about life after death. (No one has studied the psyche as much or as long as the Hindus.) In the late 1800s, some Hindu texts, written in Sanskrit, were starting to be translated into English. (Some Sanskrit words are used herein because there are no equivalent words in English.)

---

[15] Annie Besant, *Man and His Bodies, Theosophical Manuals,* No. 7 (1896; repr., London: Theosophical Publishing House, 1971), 61.

As you read what follows, you may want to refer to the diagram at the end of this chapter. You will notice there are seven planes, each of which has seven subplanes, ordered according to vibrational frequency. The lowest (and densest) level is the physical plane where liquids and solids and gases are found. At death, the soul will travel from the physical to the etheric plane and then onward until it reaches the causal plane.[16]

THEOSOPHICAL TEACHINGS ABOUT DEATH AND REBIRTH

Theosophy instructs that we have many bodies (physical, etheric, astral, and mental). At death, our soul expression departs the physical body but retains the invisible bodies for varying lengths of time as the soul moves from plane to plane. Leaving the physical plane, the soul moves to the astral plane, then to the mental plane, and then, upon reaching the soul/causal plane, it plans the next incarnation.

When the soul is ready to assume a new personality, the etheric, astral, and mental sheaths that were previously released are again taken on. These bodies hold the experiences of previous lifetimes.

Theosophical teachings are quite different from the Christian notions of Heaven and Hell and provide a much richer and more purposeful view of the after-death experience. (Belief in reincarnation by the early Christians was largely dropped

---

[16] Different authors will use different names for the seven planes of existence. These planes are not so much places as states of being.

by the fourth century. Christian teachings were determined by the Roman Catholic Church after that time, and the Church did not accept the idea of reincarnation.)

What follows is a more detailed look at the process of death and rebirth.

ETHERIC PLANE

After the death of the physical body, the consciousness focal point shifts to the etheric body. According to Annie Besant, the *Linga Sharira*, or *astral double*, is the ethereal counterpart of the gross body of man.

> During the slow process of dying, while the Linga Sharira is withdrawing from the body, as after it has withdrawn, extreme quiet and self-control should be observed in the chamber of Death. For during this time, the whole life passes swiftly in review before the Ego, as those have related who have passed in drowning into this unconscious and pulseless state. This is the time during which the thought-images of the ended earth-life, clustering around their maker, group and interweave themselves into the completed image of that life, and

are impressed in their totality on the Astral Light.[17]

In *Man and His Bodies,* Annie Besant describes the release of the etheric body which usually occurs within seventy-two hours:

> In sleep the thinking Ego slips out of these two bodies, or rather one body with its visible and invisible parts, leaving them together; in death it slips out for the last time, but with this difference, that it draws out the etheric double with it, separating from its dense counterpart and thus rendering impossible any further play of the life-breath in the latter as an organic whole. The Ego quickly shakes off the etheric double, which as we have seen, cannot pass on to the astral plane, and leaves it to disintegrate with its lifelong partner.[18]

After releasing of the etheric body, the soul moves to the astral plane.

---

[17] Annie Besant, *Death – and After?, Theosophical Manuals,* No. 3 (London: Theosophical Publishing Society, 1893), 22–23.

Astral light, in this case, refers to the upper astral plane, the storehouse of all things, including the emotions. It holds and records past and present events of our Earth life in the "tablet" of the unseen universe.

[18] Besant, *Man and His Bodies,* 28.

ASTRAL PLANE

Consciousness remains on the astral plane for a time, processing, until all desires and feelings accumulated in our life experience have been depleted. (The more work we do in processing our feelings and emotions during our lifetime, the less time we will spend on the astral plane.)

According to Theosophy, most souls experience release of the etheric body soon after death and pass directly to the middle astral plane or intermediate level. Souls in need of redemption because of their evil conduct enter the lower astral plane. The concept of purgatory bears some similarity to the Eastern idea of the lower astral plane, which is a hellish state. (In Roman Catholic theology, purgatory is an intermediate state where some of the souls destined for Heaven must first go for purification.)

Very evil souls may go to the Avitchi, described by A. P. Sinnett as a place of annihilation.[19] These souls will only be able to reenter the life cycle at the beginning of the next Earth cycle, which could be millions of Earth years, thus delaying soul development and growth.[20]

---

[19] A. P. Sinnett, *Esoteric Buddhism* (Boston: Houghton, Mifflin and Company, 1884), 129.

[20] Our planet has gone through a number of incarnations, just as each of us go through different incarnations. Earth has gone through the Saturn, Sun, and Moon cycles and is now in the Earth cycle. In the future, Earth will go through the Jupiter, Venus, and Vulcan cycles. In the Saturn period, man was created as a divine spark of essence by God. During the Vulcan period, man will transcend to the spirit body and will be able to see into the spirit realm. More information may be found in *Cosmic Memory: Prehistory of Earth and Man* by Rudolf Steiner.

MENTAL/DEVACHAN PLANE

When the release of the astral body is complete, the soul exists on the *mental/Devachan plane*, the arena of our thoughts. The time spent here is longer, possibly hundreds of years.

On the mental/Devachan plane, the soul experiences and processes the thoughts that were generated during the earthly life. The knowledge and wisdom that have been accumulated are carried forward to this plane.

Esoteric Buddhism provides an introduction to the mental/Devachan plane.

> That which survives in Devachan is not merely the individual monad, which survives through all the changes of the whole evolutionary scheme, and flits from body to body, from planet to planet, and so forth, — that which survives in Devachan is the man's own self-conscious personality.[21]

In esoteric thought, the soul is much greater than the personality. (The soul is ever evolving toward perfection. Upon achieving enlightenment, even the soul body is released and a still higher state is attained (called the *monad*) in which consciousness abides in the *atman* or divine plane in conjunction with buddhi, i.e. soul.)

In *Man and His Bodies*, Annie Besant describes the process of leaving the mental/Devachan plane to move on to the soul/causal plane as follows:

---

[21] Sinnett, *Esoteric Buddhism*, 124.

But from this mind body also he withdraws when the time is ripe, taking from it to carry on into the body that endures the essence of all that he has gathered and assimilated. He leaves the mind body behind him, to disintegrate after the fashion of his denser vehicles, for the matter of it — subtle as it is from our standpoint — is not subtle enough to pass onward to the higher planes of the manasic world. It has to be shaken off, to be left to go back into the materials of its own region, once more a resolution of the combinations into its elements. All the way up man is shaking off body after body, and only on reaching the arupa planes of the manasic world can he be said to have passed beyond the regions over which the disintegrating sceptre of Death has sway. He passes finally out of his dominions, dwelling in the causal body over which Death has no power, and in which he stores up all that he has gathered. Hence its very name of causal body, since all causes that affect future incarnations reside in it.[22]

The personality we adopted for this current lifetime does not continue from life to life. It drops away in the mental/ Devachan plane to make way for a new personality. (The new

---

[22] Besant, *Man and His Bodies*, 110.

personality that is chosen will be appropriate for the life lessons planned for the next incarnation.)

SOUL/CAUSAL PLANE

Upon leaving the mental/Devachan plane, the essence of the knowledge and wisdom gained in the previous life and lifetimes moves with the soul to the soul/causal plane. These characteristics will be carried forward into the next incarnation.

C. W. Leadbeater, an early member of the Theosophical Society, discussed the purpose of incarnating into a physical body in *The Life After Death:*

> You are here for a purpose — a purpose which can only be attained upon this physical plane. The soul has to take much trouble, to go through much limitation, in order to gain this earthly incarnation, and therefore its efforts must not be thrown away unnecessarily. The instinct of self-preservation is divinely implanted in our breasts, and it is our duty to make the most of this earthly life which is ours, and to retain it as long as circumstances permit. There are lessons to be learnt on this plane which cannot be learnt anywhere else, and the sooner we learn them the sooner we shall be free for ever from the need of return to this lower and more limited life. So none must dare to die until this

time comes, though when it does come he may well rejoice, for indeed he is about to pass from labour to refreshment.[23]

Life and death and rebirth repeat until we reach enlightenment and no longer need to return in a new incarnation.

BUDDHIC PLANE

Upon reaching enlightenment, the soul enters the *buddhic plane*, a state of pure consciousness. At the level of achievement called Buddhahood or Christ Consciousness, a choice arises within the soul of whether to take an individual path forward for continued soul growth or to return in new incarnations to help the suffering world.

A student of the Theosophical teacher Gottfried de Purucker asked about the value of dwelling on life's sorrows and wondered if choosing to focus on that which is beautiful and "sweet" is selfish and cowardly. Gottfried de Purucker replied:

> Your question is a profound one. You have stated in it the problem which every human being will someday have to solve. You have set forth to your own consciousness the choice which one day we all have to make. It is this, which path shall we follow; the path of peace and happiness

---

[23] C. W. Leadbeater, *The Life After Death* (1912; repr., Adyar, India: Theosophical Publishing House, 1998), 28–29.

for self alone, the path of the Pratyeka-Buddhas — a holy path, to be sure, a beautiful path, yes — or shall we, on the other hand, choose the path of self-renunciation for the world, a path of sublimity, a path of personal sorrow, but nevertheless a path with the sunlight of eternity shining upon it, and with the reward of the gods awaiting us after long aeons.

The Buddhas of Compassion are, really, far holier than the Pratyeka-Buddhas. The Buddhas of Compassion live for the world. They renounce everything of a selfish character. They give up their own spiritual goals in order to return along the path so that they can help their fellow-beings who are less progressed than they themselves. But while doing so, they live nevertheless in the glory and beauty of life. They live in the light. Their own inner life is a beacon of Divine light.[24]

As the Buddhas of Compassion choose to return and live in the world again to help mankind, so did Krishna and Jesus say they will come again. The Divine will incarnate anew.

---

[24] Gottfried de Purucker, *The Dialogues of G. de Purucker: Report of Sessions, Katherine Tingley Memorial Group*, vol. 3, ed. Arthur L. Conger (Pasadena, CA: Theosophical University Press, 1948), 82–83.

NIRVANIC PLANE

Upon leaving the buddhic plane, the soul moves to the nirvanic plane, the highest human aspect of soul expression. The nirvanic consciousness belongs to those who have completed the life cycle of human evolution and who are called Masters.

What lies on the planes beyond the nirvanic plane (paranirvanic and mahaparanirvanic) is hidden in the unimaginable light of God.

From this overview, we can see that consciousness continues throughout all the planes of existence. Through a process of reincarnation, the soul evolves toward perfection over the course of many lifetimes until it reaches Nirvana. (Few of us reach the level of sainthood in one lifetime.) Enlightenment is an attainable human goal and one worth striving towards, thus giving all humans a purpose or reason for being.

PLANES OF NATURE

7	**MAHÂPARANIRVÂNIC**	FIRST	TRIPLE MANIFESTATION ◯ ◯ ◯	
6	**PARANIRVÂNIC**		SECOND ◯ ◯	
5	**NIRVÂNIC**	ATOMIC	THIRD ✠	
		SPIRIT	THREEFOLD SPIRIT in MAN ✷ ✷ ✷	
4	**BUDDHIC**	ATOMIC		
		The Reincarnating Ego or Soul in Man	INTUITION ✷ ✷	
3	**MENTAL** ARUPA	ATOMIC	INTELLIGENCE CAUSAL BODY ✷	
	RUPA		MENTAL BODY	
2	**ASTRAL**	ATOMIC	ASTRAL BODY	
1	**PHYSICAL**	ATOMIC SUB-ATOMIC SUPER-ETHERIC ETHERIC	ETHERIC DOUBLE	
		GASEOUS LIQUID SOLID	DENSE BODY	

The diagram has been reprinted with permission from:

Man Visible and Invisible, C. W. Leadbeater, 1942, Planes of Nature, Illustration II, between page 26 and 27. This image was reproduced by permission of Quest Books, the imprint of The Theosophical Publishing House (www. questbooks.net).

Note: For more information on the various planes, refer to the following books by A. E. Powell:

The Etheric Double and Allied Phenomena (1925)
The Astral Body and Other Astral Phenomena (1925)
The Mental Body (1927)
The Causal Body and the Ego (1928)

CHAPTER 12

CONCLUSION: WHAT NOW?

This book is a brief summary of my experiences and practices. Maybe you do not have a burning passion but only a curiosity about spirituality. Nevertheless, I hope this book has been informative.

Each person is traveling along a path toward greater spiritual awareness. Whether in this life or another, we will each awaken and pursue truth and wisdom. Practice meditation and learn to hear that still small voice within, trusting that messages from your higher self are given for your highest good.

In the Appendix I have included several lists of books I recommend for your spiritual development. You may also wish to refer to the bibliography for works cited in this book.

By going within to connect with the Divine and the universal consciousness, you can go beyond intellect. I suggest you start by creating a meditation space in your home.

Utilizing the spiritual sense of taste, decorate your sanctuary with art that is meaningful to you and provides inspiration. Fill your library with self-help books and/or books about spirituality. There are many authors that write encouraging, inspirational material.

Look for God in nature. Take a walk outside in the park or forest or along the beach. Being near water, especially, is a healing, cleansing way to refresh your spirit.

If you have a dark-night-of-the-soul experience, don't resist the changes that are occurring in your inner and outer life. When everything that is no longer essential has been stripped away, what remains is a strong connection to God.

Don't live in fear of death. Consciousness continues beyond death.

Get to know your spirit guides and teachers. Form a relationship. Communicate often. They are there with you to teach and guide you.

Love answers all calls. Practice love and compassion and your life will turn out all right.

Your God, by any name, dwells within you. Trust that presence.

Honor the life you have been given with gratitude and appreciation. Take moments to be reverent of your Divine essence. Develop tolerance for other beliefs.

Live as if you were on fire with divine purpose. Help others. Make a difference in the world.

The spiritual path can be lonely. Many are called, but few answer the call. Find a mentor. Look for wise spiritual pioneers who are willing to share their insight with interested listeners.

When you have sufficient knowledge and wisdom, become a teacher. Share your gifts and knowledge with those around you. Everyone is a teacher. We are either teaching what to do or what not to do. Someone is watching you and learning from you.

The first place to look for unconditional love is within ourselves. If we can love, cherish, and forgive ourselves and others, we can handle life's difficulties.

MANTRA

I am filled with Light.
I walk in the Light.
I practice Light work.
I am Light.

APPENDIX

RECOMMENDED READING LISTS FOR SELF-GUIDED SPIRITUAL DEVELOPMENT

Reading the accounts of those who have traveled into the spiritual realm can help to demystify these experiences, which are natural and should not cause fright. A good place to start is with the writings of Emanuel Swedenborg and Helena Blavatsky. These two mystics have written extensively about their psychic and otherworldly experiences.

If you are interested in *nature spirits*, a good resource to consult is *The Kingdom of the Gods* by Geoffrey Hodson (1972).

The following reading lists are given in order of difficulty.

Foundational Reading List to Facilitate Your Spiritual Path

The Impersonal Life by Anonymous (1941)

The Sermon on the Mount by Emmet Fox (1932)

The Prophet by Kahlil Gibran (1923)

Light from Many Lamps by Lillian Eichler Watson (1951)

Self-Unfoldment by Disciplines of Realization by Manly P. Hall (1942)

The Way of the Wizard: Twenty Spiritual Lessons for Creating the Life You Want by Deepak Chopra (1995)

The Ten Commandments by Emmet Fox (1953)

The Way to the Kingdom by Joseph Benner (1988)

Revelation: The Road to Overcoming by Charles Neal (2000)

In Tune with the Infinite by Ralph Waldo Trine (1908)

Intermediate I Reading
List for Spiritual Study

The Mystical Christ by Manly P. Hall (1993)

Old Testament Wisdom by Manly P. Hall (1987)

Living in the Light by Shakti Gawain (1986)

The Power of Your Subconscious Mind by Joseph Murphy (1963)

The Twelve Powers of Man by Charles Fillmore (1995)

Words to the Wise by Manly P. Hall (1963)

The Medicine Way by Kenneth Meadows (1997)

The Seat of the Soul by Gary Zukav (1989)

The Road Less Traveled by M. Scott Peck, M.D. (1978)

The Power of Awareness by Neville (1952)

She: Understanding Feminine Psychology by Robert A. Johnson (1989)

He: Understanding Masculine Psychology by Robert A. Johnson (1977)

The Magic of Thinking Big by David Schwartz (1979)

Intermediate II Reading List for Spiritual Study

The Way of Life According to Lao Tzu by Witter Bynner (1986)

The Edinburgh Lectures on Mental Science by Thomas Troward (1909)

Pathways of Philosophy by Manly P. Hall (1947)

The Phoenix by Manly P. Hall (1975)

The Woman's Dictionary of Symbols and Sacred Objects by Barbara Walker (1988)

Spiritual Centers in Man by Manly P. Hall (1978)

Twelve World Teachers by Manly P. Hall (1965)

The Master Key by Charles F. Haanel (1919)

The Science of Mind by Ernest Holmes (1938)

Seven Taoist Masters by Eva Wong (1990)

Thundering Silence by Thich Nhat Hanh (1993)

Intermediate III Reading List for Spiritual Study

The Secret Teachings of All Ages by Manly P. Hall (1975)

The Way of the Shaman by Michael Harner (1980)

Free Play by Stephen Nachmanovitch (1990)

Laws of Hermetic Wisdom by Robert Thibodeau (1978)

At the Feet of the Master by Alcyone (Jiddu Krishnamurti) (1927)

Zohar: The Book of Splendor: Basic Readings from the Kabbalah by Gershom Scholem (1949)

The Women of Israel by Grace Aguilar (2003)

Three Remarkable Women by Harold Balyoz (1986)

The Kybalion: Hermetic Philosophy by Three Initiates (1940)

Advanced Reading List
for Spiritual Study

Anacalypsis by Godfrey Higgins Volume I and Volume II (1836)

Melchizedek Truth Principles by Frater Achad (1963)

Life between Death and Rebirth by Rudolf Steiner (1968)

Knowledge of the Higher Worlds and Its Attainment by Rudolf Steiner (1986)

An Outline of Occult Science by Rudolf Steiner (1972)

Ancient Mystical White Brotherhood by Frater Achad (1976)

Your Forces and How to Use Them by C. D. Larson (1971)

The Soul and its Mechanism by Alice Bailey (1950)

A Treatise on Cosmic Fire by Alice Bailey (1973)

The Secret Doctrine of the Rosicrucians by Magus Incognito (1949)

Morals and Dogma by Albert Pike (1966)

Questions and Answers by Manly P. Hall (1965)

The Rosicrucian Cosmo-Conception or Mystic Christianity by Max Heindel (1973)

The Secret Doctrine by H. P. Blavatsky Volume I and Volume II (1888)

Isis Unveiled by H. P. Blavatsky Volume I and Volume II (1988)

GLOSSARY

Akashic records   A compendium of all human events, past, present, and future, including thoughts, words, emotions, and intentions.

apparition   A ghost or ghostlike image of a person.

astral double   The counterpart or shadow of man or animal in spirit.

astral plane   One of seven planes of existence where consciousness focuses after death of the physical body before going on to the higher spheres, usually thought of as a place to process and release our emotions and desires.

atman   Sanskrit word that means divine self; pure consciousness, which is a part of us.

atmic plane   Beyond the buddhic plane of existence is the atmic plane where freedom and bliss are experienced.

auric egg	Physically, though invisibly, the human auric envelope that surrounds a person. The auric egg endures from life to life and preserves the karmic causes and effects generated by individuals during their previous incarnations.
Avitchi	The lowest level of Hell.
buddhic plane	Beyond the soul/causal plane of existence is the buddhic plane where the buddhi (i.e. soul) exists. All those who continually stand in the light of the soul on the buddhic plane are considered Masters.
chakras	Centers of spiritual power within the human body through which energy flows, usually pictured as seven main wheels along the spine.
clairaudience	Perceiving and hearing with the inner ear what is inaudible to the physical ears.
claircognizance	The intuitive ability of clear knowing.
clairsentience	An ability to feel the emotions of people, animals, and spirits.
clairvoyance	The ability to perceive events in the future.
déjà vu	A feeling of familiarity, as if one has already experienced something without an identifiable reason.
dark night of the soul	A crisis in life that brings us to our knees and humbles us.
dharma	Essential quality of one's own nature.

discarnate entity	A person who has died or an entity in spirit with only a very subtle physical body that ordinarily cannot be seen by the physical eyes.
dukkha	Suffering, sorrow, pain, imperfection, impermanence.
esoteric	Obscure knowledge likely to be understood only by a few.
ESP	Extrasensory perception, or our sixth sense or second sight, includes reception of information not gained through recognized physical senses but sensed by the mind.
etheric body	The closest subtle body to our physical body. The etheric body sustains the physical body. The Sanskrit term is Linga Sharira.
hierophant	In ancient Greece, a person, especially a priest or a bishop, who interpreted sacred mysteries or esoteric principles.
intuition	The ability to acquire knowledge without proof, evidence, or conscious reasoning or without understanding how the knowledge was acquired.
kundalini	A form of primal energy that lies dormant at the base of the spine and can move up the spine during spiritual awakening.
Linga Sharira	The invisible double of the human body, also known as the etheric body, doppelganger, or bioplasmic body. This body is considered to contain all vital functions. It keeps the physical body alive.

mental/Devachan plane	A world of thought. The plane where souls go after the astral plane.
monad	Refers to atman (pure eternal Spirit) and buddhi (the soul), which serves as the vehicle through which the divine light and radiance of Atma shines through to the perceiving mind. Spirit is the vitality of the soul.
nature spirits	Spirits of the elements; part of the elemental kingdom. These spirits inhabit nature and help support and heal Earth, under the general designation of fairies.
Neo-Theosophy	A system of theosophical ideas expounded by Annie Besant and Charles W. Leadbeater after the death of Helena Blavatsky.
Nirvana	Transcendent state where one is released from all desire and suffering, ending the cycle of birth and death and karma.
No Mind	A Zen concept. Mind without thought. A state of mind not fixed or occupied by thought or emotion and thus open to everything. Also, a meditative therapy practiced by Osho.
numinous	Arousing spiritual or religious emotion; awe-inspiring, mysterious.
oneness	Awareness of the force in consciousness that unifies the whole timeless universe as one Divine creation.
paranormal	Supernatural perception without scientific explanation.

prana	Life force, life energy, vital principle.
psyche	A Greek word for the human soul, mind, and spirit.
psychometry	The power to perceive information from an object about its owner through extrasensory perception.
Sanskrit	The primary liturgical language of Hinduism. An ancient Indic language, in which the Hindu scriptures are written and from which many northern Indian languages are derived.
sentient	Any living creature. A sentient being is one who perceives and responds to sensations of whatever kind — sight, hearing, touch, taste, or smell. Sentience is the capacity to feel, perceive, or experience subjectively.
shaman/shamanism	Spiritual leaders within indigenous cultures. They are capable of entering an altered state to move into the unseen world. An ancient healing tradition, shamanism is a way to connect with nature and all of creation.
soul	The immaterial essence, animating principle, and actuating cause. The soul stores our lifetimes of knowledge and experience. The human soul has a divine essence.

soul/causal plane	The plane beyond the mental plane where souls prepare for their next incarnation. The plane on which the wisdom, positive experiences, and successes accumulated in the soul's previous lifetimes are stored.
spirit	As used in this book, spirit refers to the realm that ordinarily cannot be seen or known with our physical senses.
spirit realms	The invisible realms where discarnate entities, aliens, angels, and other beings exist. Visions and messages may come to us from the unseen realms.
spiritual emergency	A psychospiritual crisis as described by psychotherapist Christina Grof and psychiatrist Stanislov Grof.
subtle realm	The invisible realm around us that is material but too fine to perceive with the naked eye.
synchronicity	The simultaneous occurrence of events that seem to be significantly related but have no discernable causal connection.
Tarot	Illustrated cards used for divination since the 18th century.
telepathy	Transmitting of information from one person to another without using any of our known sensory channels or physical interaction.
Theosophist	One with mystical insight into the nature of the Divine. Also, members of the Theosophical Society.

vibrational states　　All creation is manifest from divine energy. The subtle bodies (etheric, astral, and mental) are less dense than the physical body and vibrate at higher frequencies. We can raise our vibration through practices that help us attain higher levels of consciousness.

BIBLIOGRAPHY

Anthony, Carol K. *A Guide to the I Ching.* Stow, MA: Anthony Publishing Company, 1982.

Besant, Annie. *Death and After? Theosophical Manuals*, No. 3. London: Theosophical Publishing Society, 1893.

————. *Man and His Bodies. Theosophical Manuals*, No. 7. 1896. Reprint, Adyar, India: Theosophical Publishing House, 1971.

Blavatsky, Helena P., trans. *The Voice of the Silence: Being Chosen Fragments from the "Book of the Golden Precepts."* Blavatsky Centenary Edition. Edmonton, Canada: Edmonton Theosophical Society, 1991.

Eliade, Mircea. *Shamanism: Archaic Techniques of Ecstasy.* Princeton, NJ: Princeton University Press, 1964.

Hall, Manly P. *Man: The Grand Symbol of the Mysteries.* 1937. Reprint, Los Angeles: Philosophical Research Society, 1972.

————. *Self-Unfoldment by Disciplines of Realization.* 1942. Reprint, Los Angeles: Philosophical Research Society, 1977.

Hay, Louise. *Heal Your Body: The Mental Causes for Physical Illness and the Metaphysical Way to Overcome Them.* Santa Monica, CA: Hay House, 1988.

Juan de la Cruz. *The Dark Night of the Soul.* Translated by Gabriela Cunninghame Graham. London: John M. Watkins, 1905.

Knoche, Grace F. *The Mystery Schools.* 1940. Reprint, Pasadena, CA: Theosophical University Press, 1999.

Leadbeater, C. W. *The Life After Death.* 1912. Reprint, Adyar, India: The Theosophical Publishing House, 1998.

Meadows, Kenneth. *Shamanic Spirit.* Santa Fe, NM: Bear & Company, 2004.

Osho. *Meditation: The First and Last Freedom.* New York: St. Martin's Press, 1996.

————. *The Song of Ecstasy: Talks on Adi Shankara's Bhaj Govindam.* Pune, India: Rebel Publishing House, 2000.

Purucker, Gottfried de. *The Dialogues of G. de Purucker: Report of Sessions, Katherine Tingley Memorial Group.* Vol. 3. Edited by Arthur L. Conger. Pasadena, CA: Theosophical University Press, 1948.

Saraydarian, Torkom. *Obsession and Possession.* Cave Creek, AZ: TSG Publishing Foundation, 2000.

Sinnett, A. P. *Esoteric Buddhism.* Boston: Houghton, Mifflin and Company, 1884.

Steiner, Rudolf. *Cosmic Memory: Prehistory of Earth and Man.* Englewood, NJ: Rudolf Steiner Publications, 1959.

Unity Worldwide Ministries. *Meditation in the Silence.* Kansas City, MO: Unity Books.

INDEX

K

kundalini 42, 43, 95

L

Linga Sharira 72, 95

M

mental/Devachan plane 75, 76, 77, 96
monad 75, 96

N

nature spirits 87, 96
Neo-theosophy 30, 96
Nirvana 80, 96
nirvanic plane 80
No Mind xxxi, 61, 65, 96
numinous 8, 23, 96

P

paranormal 59, 96
prana 29, 97
psyche 30, 34, 36, 70, 97
psychometry 28, 97

R

Reptilians xxviii, 43

S

Sanskrit 29, 70, 93, 95, 97
sentient 56, 57, 97
shaman 45, 46, 91, 97

shamanic xxiv, 17, 41, 43, 45, 46, 102
shamanism 38, 45, 46, 97, 101
soul/causal plane 71, 75, 77, 94, 98
spirit guides xx, xxiv, 47, 48, 49, 50, 51, 69, 84
spirit realm 13, 19, 21, 22, 59, 74, 98
spiritual abuse xxiv, 33
spiritual emergency 17, 41, 43, 98
subtle xx, 28, 29, 76, 95, 98, 99
synchronicity 98

T

Tarot 42, 98
telepathy 12, 98
Theosophist 50, 70, 98

V

vibrational states 99